Advanced

FANTASIA DI FALCONE

for Euphonium and Piano
James Curnow

CURNOW® MUSIC

EXCLUSIVELY DISTRIBUTED BY

HAL•LEONARD® CORPORATION
7777 W. BLUEMOUND RD. P.O. BOX 13819 MILWAUKEE, WI 53213

Edition Number: CMP 1068-06-401

FANTASIA DI FALCONE
for Euphonium and Piano
James Curnow

ISBN 978-90-431-2464-8

James Curnow

James Curnow was born in Port Huron, Michigan and raised in Royal Oak, Michigan. He lives in Nicholasville, Kentucky where he is president, composer, and educational consultant for Curnow Music Press, Inc. of Lexington, Kentucky, publishers of significant music for concert band and brass band. He also serves as Composer-in-residence (Emeritus) on the faculty of Asbury College in Wilmore, Kentucky, and is editor of all music publications for The Salvation Army in Atlanta, Georgia.

His formal training was received at Wayne State University (Detroit, Michigan) and at Michigan State University (East Lansing, Michigan), where he was a euphonium student of Leonard alcone, and a conducting student of Dr. Harry Begian. His studies in composition and arranging were with F. Maxwell Wood, James Gibb, Jere Hutchinson, and Irwin Fischer.

James Curnow has taught in all areas of instrumental music, both in the public schools (five years), and on the college and university level (twenty-six years). He is a member of several professional organizations, including the American Bandmasters Association, College Band Directors National Association, World Association of Symphonic Bands and Wind Ensembles and the American Society of Composers, Authors and Publishers (ASCAP). In 1980 he received the National Band Association's Citation of Excellence. In 1985, while a tenured Associate Professor at the University of Illinois, Champaign-Urbana, Mr. Curnow was honored as an outstanding faculty member. Among his most recent honors are inclusion in Who's Who in America, Who's Who in the South and Southwest, and Composer of the Year (1997) by the Kentucky Music Teachers Association and the National Music Teachers Association. He has received annual ASCAP standard awards since 1979.

As a conductor, composer and clinician, Curnow has traveled throughout the United States, Canada, Australia, Japan and Europe where his music has received wide acclaim. He has won several awards for band compositions including the ASBDA/Volkwein Composition Award in 1977 (Symphonic Triptych) and 1979 (Collage for Band), the ABA/Ostwald Award in 1980 (Mutanza) and 1984 (Symphonic Variants for Euphonium and Band), the 1985 Sixth International Competition of Original Compositions for Band (Australian Variants Suite), and the 1994 Coup de Vents Composition Competition of Le Havre, France (Lochinvar).

Curnow has been commissioned to write over two hundred works for concert band, brass band, orchestra, choir and various vocal and instrumental ensembles. His published works now number well over four hundred. His most recent commissions include the Tokyo Symphony Orchestra (Symphonic Variants for Euphonium and Orchestra), the United States Army Band (Pershing's Own, Washington, D.C.-Lochinvar, Symphonic Poem for Winds and Percussion), Roger Behrend and the DEG Music Products, Inc. and Willson Band Instrument Companies (Concerto for Euphonium and Orchestra), the Olympic Fanfare and Theme for the Olympic Flag (Atlanta Committee for the Olympic Games, 1996), the Kentucky Music Teachers Association/National Music Teachers Association in 1997 (On Poems of John Keats for String Quartet) and Michigan State University Bands (John Whitwell, Director of Bands) in honor of David Catron's twenty-six years of service to the university and the university bands (Ode And Epinicion).

FANTASIA DI FALCONE
for Euphonium and Piano

James Curnow (ASCAP)

Program Note

Dedicated to Mrs. Leonard (Beryl) Falcone on the 20th anniversary of the Leonard Falcone International Euphonium and Tuba competition, 2005. Beryl has been an avid supporter of musicians, from the beginning of their studies throughout their lives. She has given unselfishly of her time and effort toward the Falcone Festival, making the annual competition the best in the United States. The Falcone Festival encourages musicianship of the highest level and through this composition offers new and exciting performance possibilities.

The title makes an obvious reference to both my teacher, mentor and renown Baritone Horn teacher/soloist Leonard Falcone, and to the title of a piece of music he transcribed for Baritone Horn, which every Falcone student has played at one time or another: *Fantasia di Concerto* by Eduardo Boccalari. *Fantasia Di Falcone* is a four movement suite of fantasy variations, based on a theme from another Falcone favorite band transcription: *Andrea Chanier* (Opera excerpts) by Umberto Giordano. This theme is only referenced (not quoted) in the opening cadenza of Movement #1, then developed throughout the overall construction of all four movements.

The four movements are as follows:

Movement I, Adagio e espressivo, Adagietto e delicate, opens with a slow expressive cadenza (unaccompanied) by the soloist, which eventually draws the piano into a dialogue between the soloist and the piano. A brief Adagietto (lighter and a bit quicker) showcases the soloist against the piano in a moderately slow, light, dance-like section before returning the opening Adagio.

Movement II, Allegro, is a fast paced, duple meter romp that features the soloist in a call and response mode with the piano.

Movement III, Andante moderato e espressivo, is as the directive states, "at a moderate walking tempo and with expression." This movement contrasts the soloist with the piano and gives the soloist many opportunities to display the beautiful tone and expressive playing of the Euphonium.

Movement IV, Scherzando, presents a very fast and delightful tour-de-force for both the soloist and the piano.

FANTASIA DI FALCONE

James Curnow (ASCAP)

for Euphonium and Piano

I

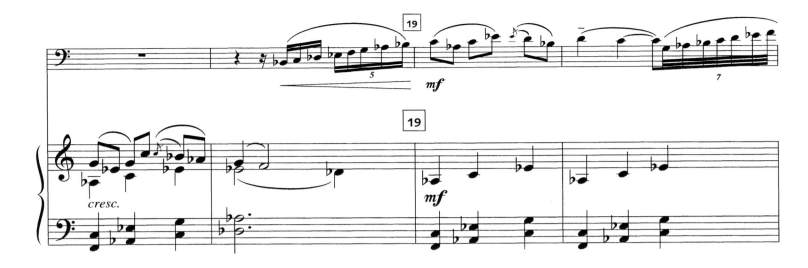

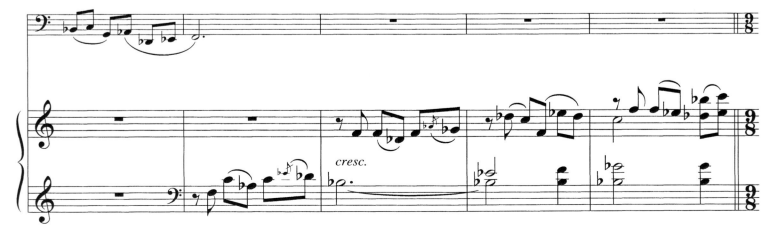

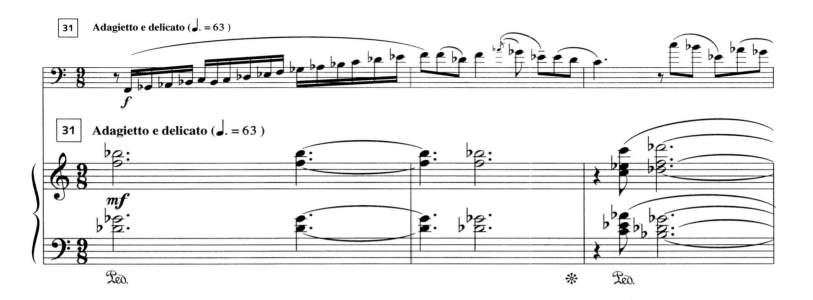

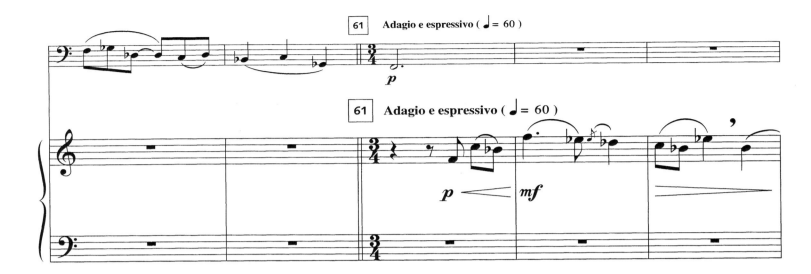

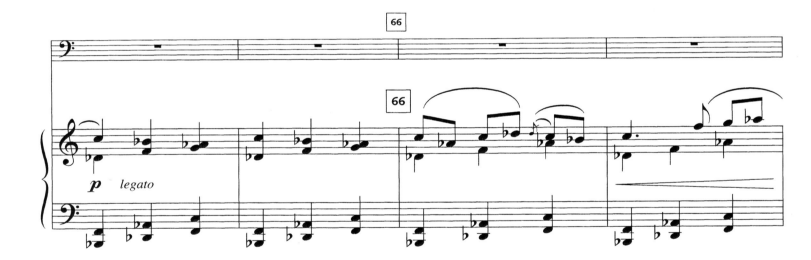

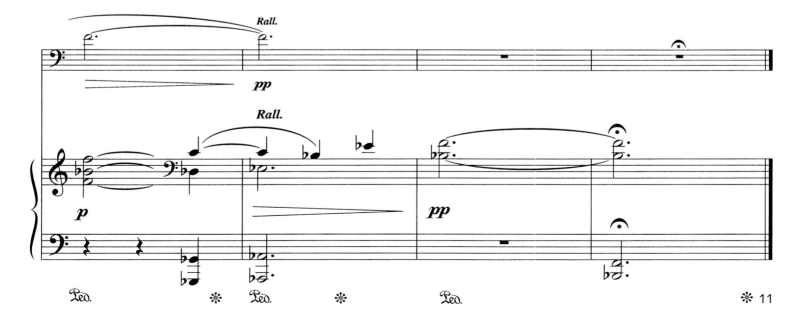

II

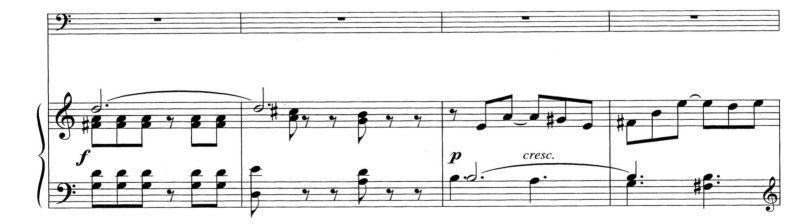

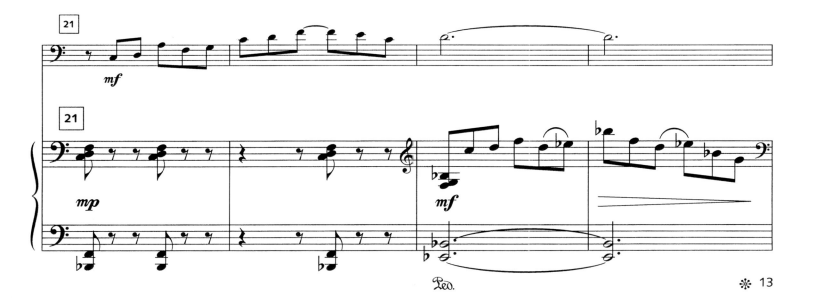

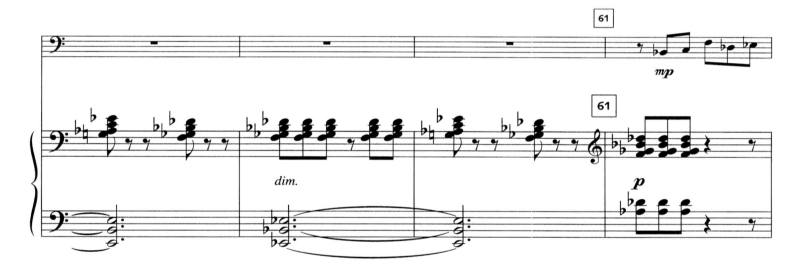

FESTIVAL SOLO SERIES

EUPHONIUM B.C. Advanced

FANTASIA DI FALCONE

for Euphonium and Piano
James Curnow

CURNOW MUSIC

EXCLUSIVELY DISTRIBUTED BY

HAL•LEONARD® CORPORATION
7777 W. BLUEMOUND RD. P.O. BOX 13819 MILWAUKEE, WI 53213

EUPHONIUM B. C.

FANTASIA DI FALCONE

James Curnow (ASCAP)

for Euphonium and Piano

I

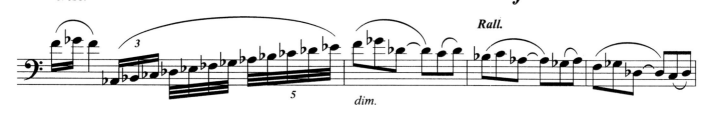

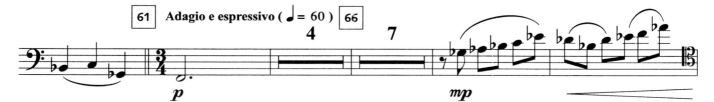

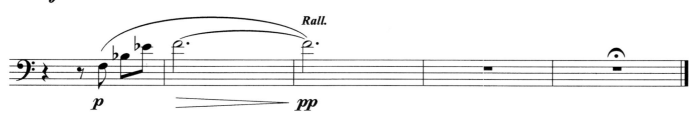

EUPHONIUM B. C.

II

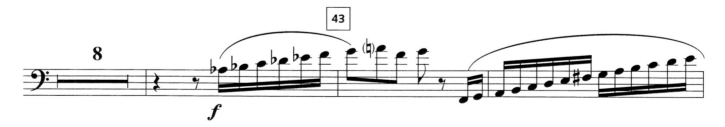

III

Andante moderato e espressivo (♩ = 60)
Sostenuto

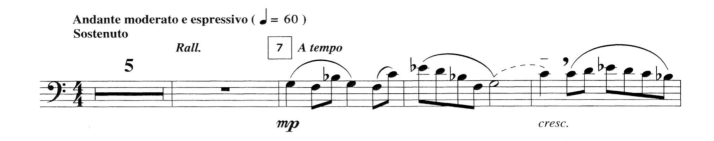

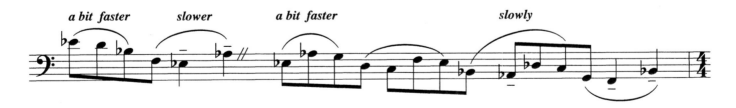

45 **Tempo primo**

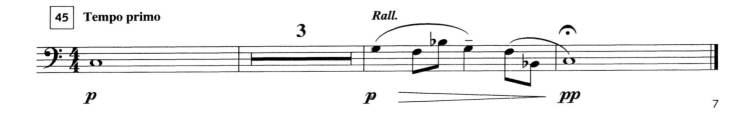

IV

EUPHONIUM T.C.   Advanced

FANTASIA DI FALCONE

for Euphonium and Piano
James Curnow

EXCLUSIVELY DISTRIBUTED BY

HAL•LEONARD®
CORPORATION

7777 W. BLUEMOUND RD. P.O. BOX 13819 MILWAUKEE, WI 53213

Bb EUPHONIUM T.C.

FANTASIA DI FALCONE

James Curnow (ASCAP)

for Euphonium and Piano

I

II

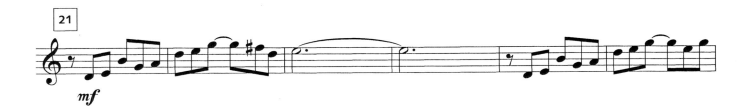

III

Andante moderato e espressivo (♩ = 60)
Sostenuto

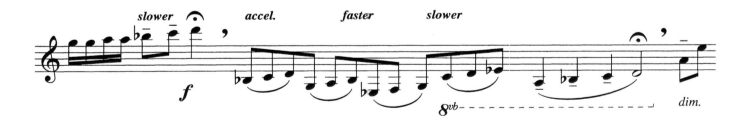

IV

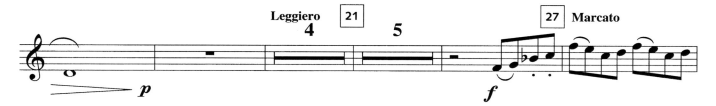

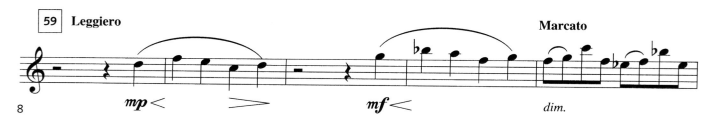

III

Pedal harmonically throughout

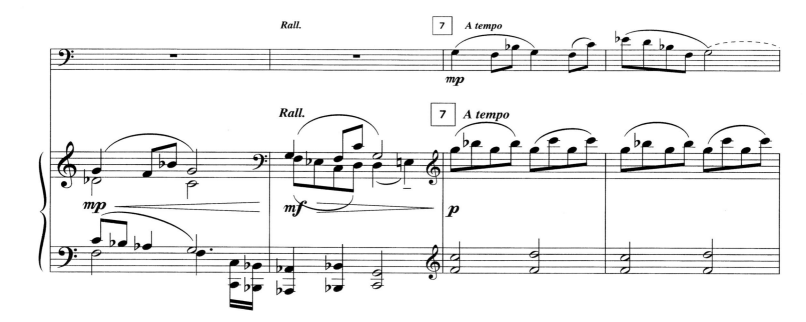

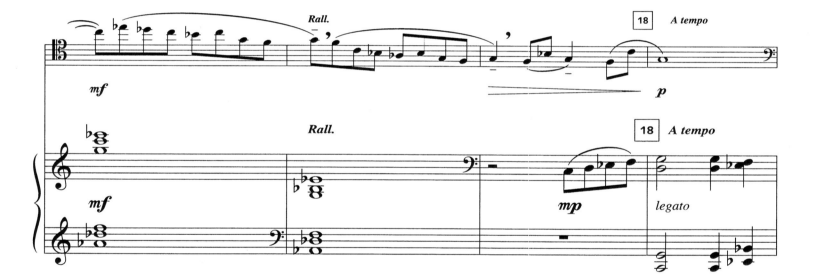

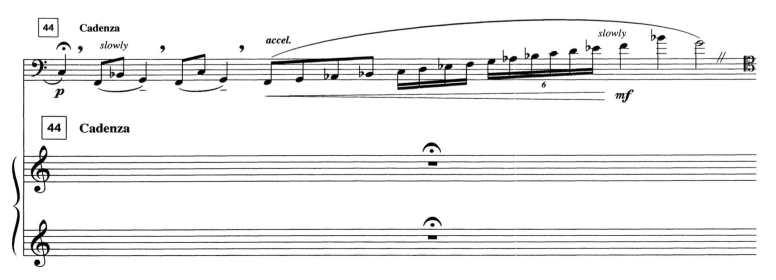

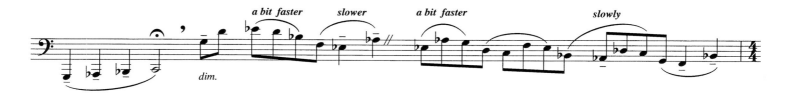

IV

26

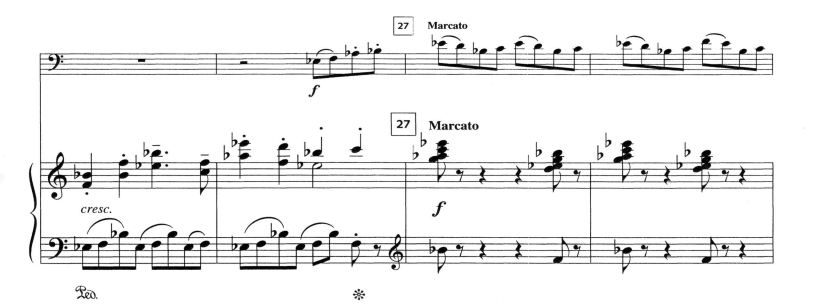

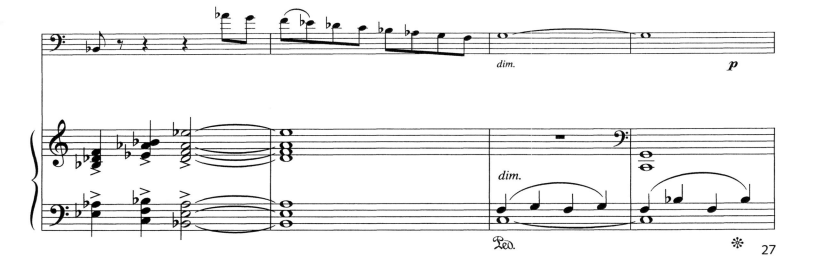

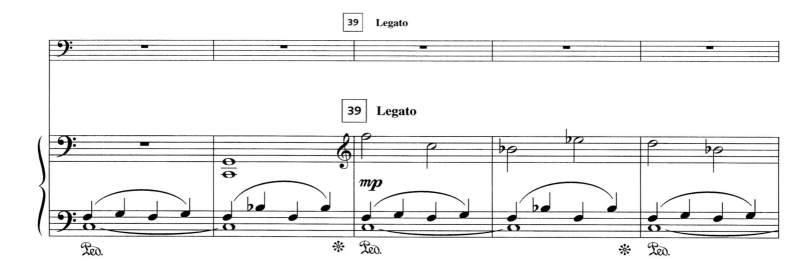

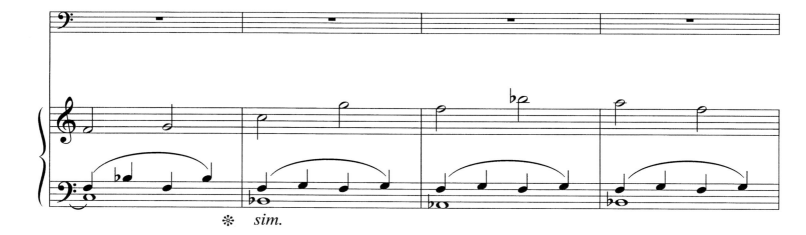

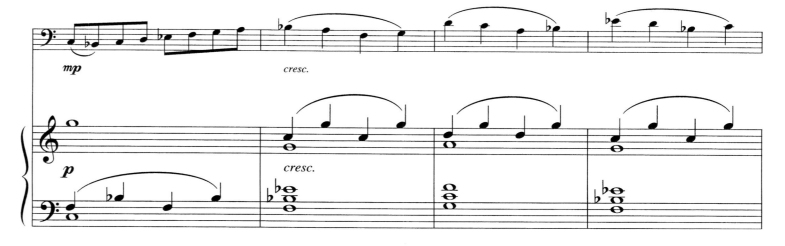

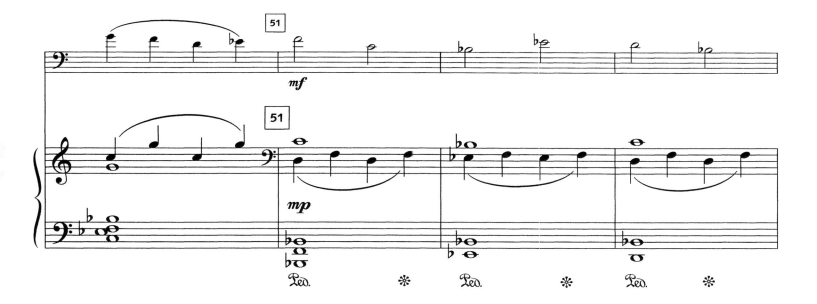

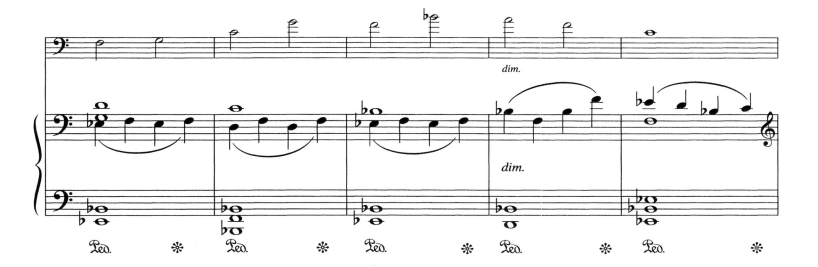

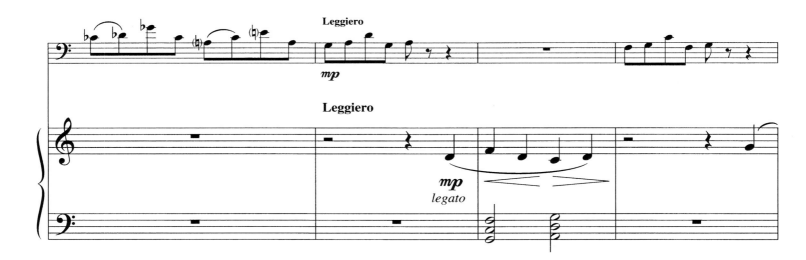

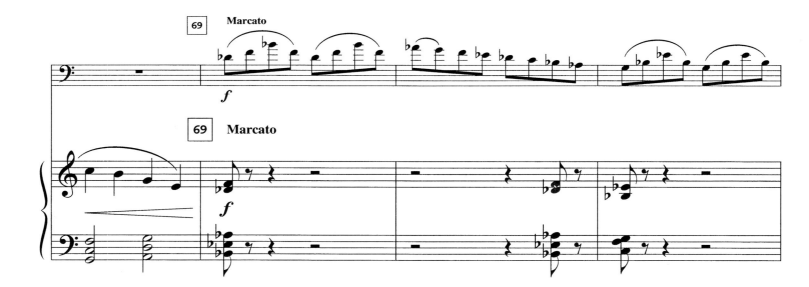

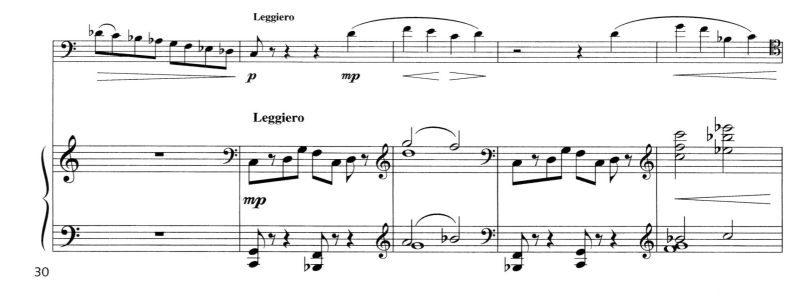